The Tow
the Country Mouse

A Folktale from Africa

Once upon a time, a country mouse had a friend from town. The country mouse sent an invitation to his friend. He asked him to come for a visit. The country mouse lived a simple life. He did not show off or put on airs. He had a small house. It was at the foot of a large tree.

The town mouse did put on airs. He called everyone "my dear fellow" or "my darling lady." He lived in the wall of a large house. He liked the hustle and bustle of town life.

Yet the invitation from the country mouse was kind. The town mouse thought about the fresh air in the country. He could get some exercise there. He packed his bag and set off for the country.

The country mouse greeted him warmly. He offered him an ear of corn for breakfast. The town mouse did not like the corn. He ate only a little of it. Then he sat back. He looked at the small house. His country friend was eating corn. He listened to the CRUNCH! CRUNCH! CRUNCH! He listened to the birds in the trees. CHIRP! CHIRP! CHIRP! It was all so boring.

"My dear fellow," the town mouse shouted. "My dear, dear fellow. . . ." He sat back and shook his head.

"What is wrong?" asked the country mouse. "You have only picked at your corn. Are you sick?"

"Not really," said the town mouse. "But I am already bored. Dear fellow, I don't see how you stand it here. It is so dull. This corn is for the birds, my dear fellow. It's not for mice. Table scraps are much better."

"What are table scraps?" asked the country mouse.

"My dear, dear fellow," said the town mouse. "You are a smart mouse. But you are a bit backward."

The town mouse shook his head sadly and jumped up.

He shouted and clapped his paws, "I've got it. Come back to town with me. I will show you a good time. There's hustle. There's bustle. There are table scraps! Come, my dear fellow. I want to show you."

The country mouse looked around his home. He tried to see it through his friend's eyes. It was small. It was quiet. He liked it very much. But those table scraps did sound interesting!

"Okay," said the country mouse. "Let's go."

And so they set out. The country mouse led the way. First, they went through the fields and hills.

Then they got near the town and hid. They sneaked into the city at night.

"Isn't this grand?" asked the town mouse.

"Uh-huh, if you say so," said the country mouse. But he looked at the trash in the gutters.

At last they came to the house. They went inside. There were huge couches in the rooms. There were beautiful rugs on the floors.

"Let's look in the dining room," whispered the town mouse.

They found the leftovers from a feast in the dining room. They ran between the legs of the table and chairs. They found tiny bits of delicious meat. They found crusts of soft bread. There were sweet crumbs. The country mouse didn't know where to begin.

The town mouse said, "See, my dear fellow, there is not even one ear of corn."

All the country mouse ever ate was corn. He stuffed himself with the good food. He thought he would burst!

He asked his friend, "How could I ever have been happy in the country?"

The town mouse smiled. Just then the door flew open. Two mean dogs ran into the room. They growled and barked. They chased the two mice. The mice escaped into a hole in the wall. That was where the town mouse lived.

Hours later it seemed safe. The town mouse whispered, "Let's get our dessert now. The dogs are gone."

The country mouse shook his head.

"Thank you for the food," he said. "But I must go back to the country now."

"What?" shouted the town mouse. "My dear fellow, life here is grand. Why must you go?"

The country mouse said, "I don't want a grand life of danger and risk. A simple life of peace and quiet is better."